Insert Praise Here!

By
Bevan Charlene McKenna

TEACH Services, Inc.
P U B L I S H I N G
www.TEACHServices.com ● (800) 367-1844

Copyright © 2015 Bevan Charlene McKenna
Copyright © 2015 TEACH Services, Inc.
ISBN-13: 978-1-4796-0065-6 (Paperback)
ISBN-13: 978-1-4796-0066-3 (ePub)
ISBN-13: 978-1-4796-0067-0 (Kindle/Mobi)
Library of Congress Control Number: 2013946466

All scripture quotations, unless otherwise indicated, are taken from the New King James Version®. Copyright © 1982 by Thomas Nelson, Inc. Used by permission. All rights reserved.

Scripture quotations marked (KJV) are taken from the King James Version Bible.

Published by

TEACH Services, Inc.
P U B L I S H I N G
www.TEACHServices.com • (800) 367-1844

Table of Contents

Introduction

Most of the experiences related in this book took place in Trinidad. Such places as Macoya Junction, Port-of-Spain, Sangre Grande, Maracas, and Jairasingh Village are all real locations in Trinidad. Colloquial expressions such as that used by Grama in Chapter 12 are also native to this country. Names of persons, for the most part, have been changed for obvious reasons. The third person has been used in some instances for dramatic effect.

All the events that have been shared in all twelve chapters are true. It is said that everyone has a story. It was my pleasure to be chosen by God to pen these stories, although it took me four years after God's initial talk with me on this to actually get busy. I can indeed *Insert Praise Here!* that

He chose me at all to have these experiences throughout my life, or to be story-keeper for my friends and my father, who permitted me to document their anecdotes as part of this tribute to God's omnipresence, omniscience, and omnipotence. It is my hope that some, if not all, of these stories resonate with you, dear readers, and that you would sense God's hand at work as He threads and weaves the events in this narrative, as well as in your own lives. At the conclusion of it all, may you encounter, recognize, and embrace every opportunity to **Insert Praise Here!**

Chapter 1

Of Baptism and Warm Water

Sabbath afternoon, August 4, was as sunny as they come. We made our way down from the crusade location in Jairasingh Village toward the site of the baptism, at the "mother church," Sangre Grande Seventh-day Adventist Church. At eight years old, I was the youngest of about seven souls who would commit our lives to Christ in baptism on that Sabbath day, harvested through the evangelistic efforts of my father, first elder of the church at the time.

For certain there was joy in heaven, as is customary on such occasions. After all, though I was born into a Seventh-day Adventist home, I was taking my own stand for God. Not only that, but there were others who were coming into the faith for the first time in their lives, albeit in their adulthood. These facts gave plenty of reasons for heaven to ring out in celebration!

As I stood before the assembly to publicly take my baptismal vows, my mind was abuzz with activity. I greatly anticipated becoming a baptized member, but I was filled with angst, for upon entering the font, I was going to face one of my biggest fears. You see, my sister had been baptized the previous September, and she had let me know that the water in the font had been ice-cold. My fear of cold water was well known by those who were close to me. So although I wanted very much to be baptized, I was terrified to enter the water. How was an eight-year-old to deal with such a tremendous obstacle?

Like all good SDA parents back then, my parents raised us on, among other things, the trusty stories of everybody's uncle, Arthur S. Maxwell. The primary lesson of these stories was always to pray and trust God to resolve any problem. Hope sprang in my mind. If God had solved the problems of those little children on the pages of those volumes, the same God could work on my behalf! I decided to put God to the test and trust Him. "God," I prayed, "you know that I am afraid of cold water. But I am going to be baptized today. You know that the water in the font is cold. Please, please send an angel to warm it up for me so that I won't be afraid. In Jesus' name, amen."

My turn came. I gingerly climbed the stairs leading into the tank, where Pastor Mitchell was waiting for me. I braced myself and hung on to my eight-year-old faith with all the trust inside me as I entered the water with no hesitation. The pastor muttered the usual words over me, and, holding my breath as I had been instructed earlier, I was plunged beneath the waters of baptism as the strains of "The cleansing stream I see, I see, I plunge, and oh, it cleanseth me" swirled around me. I walked out into the waiting arms of a deaconess, who led me to the girls' changing room.

Later on, as I walked in the church yard on my way to reenter the building, I met up with Andrew, one of the adults who had been baptized earlier that afternoon. I asked him about his experience, and he said he was glad to have been baptized. Then came the important question: "How did you find the water in the font? Cold?"

"That water was as cold as ice!" Andrew replied.

I marveled at this revelation. Then I let him know that when I had been baptized the water was as warm as could be. Not room-temperature warm, not scorching hot, but as warm as if left out in the sun. I'd like to think of it as Son-warmed! Indeed, I had had my own little miracle that day.

Over the years I have told that story to those who were willing to hear it. I have embraced a God-given mission to let my students know that God is real and can be trusted. My most recent audience, a fellow teacher, said she felt chills as I related this vignette to her on the eve of our annual school baptismal rally. I say, *Insert Praise Here!* For God is indeed real and can be trusted. God proved Himself to an eight-year-old girl one Sabbath afternoon, all those years ago, in a manner that I have been unable to forget!

If God could come through for me in what seems such an inconsequential matter, if He could show up in a little eight-year-old baptismal candidate's font and warm the water just for her, how much more will He "show Himself strong" and "do exceedingly abundantly above all that we [can] ask or think" (2 Chron. 16:9; Eph. 3:20)! If only we let Him …

Chapter 2

The Hem of His Garment?

We were heading west on the thorough-fare toward Port-of-Spain, the capital of Trinidad and Tobago, that workday morning. The maxi-taxi (a minivan carrying paying passengers), bearing its red stripes that signified its right to run fares along the East-West Corridor (the stretch from Sangre Grande in the northeast of Trinidad to Port-of-Spain in the northwest), jostled its way through the morning rush hour.

I sat in one of the front passenger seats, not wanting to be crowded in with the rest of passengers in the back. From my seat I had a clear view of the road ahead of us, of the mishmash of harried travelers swishing and swerving their way into the city.

Nothing could have prepared me for what happened next. As we approached Macoya Junction, a car, not following the rules of the road, suddenly darted out northward and turned west into the traffic, cutting in front of the maxi that I was in. And on my side, at that!

There was nothing the driver could do. The offending driver had not even given my driver the courtesy of the 10-second required reaction time. I can still hear the gasps of the other passengers as they braced themselves for impact. I could barely talk, let alone breathe. I don't even remember if it was just a thought; all I remember was being able to squeeze out a "Jesus!"

But guess what? That was about all I needed, because it was as if everything went into slow motion in that instant. I became privy to watching God at work in a way that left nothing to my imagination. While I was yet speaking, or thinking—God has that one on file—I saw a flash of white. No, it wasn't like light. It was like the tail of a white gown in motion. Trust me; I know

12

what I saw! I glimpsed it for only a brief moment, but it seemed to me to be the tail of an angel's garment—a traveling angel's garment, the one belonging to the angel who intercepted the offending car and the maxi that I was in, preventing what might have been a fatal accident. The driver of the maxi, albeit with much screeching, was able to brake; the offending driver kept on going. All of this happened in around three seconds tops!

Some may argue (judging from the outcome) that there had to have been enough time for the maxi to stop, or that the irate but relieved passengers who cussed afterward were right in doing so, or even that we were all very lucky. But I say, *Insert Praise Here!* because God sent His angel to encamp around those who feared Him to deliver them (Ps. 34:7). I know personally that He kept His word, because before I could call He answered, and while I was yet speaking, He heard (Isa. 65:24).

Take your own spin on this anecdote. Whatever you decide, know that the God who sent His angel to protect us that morning is still able to be the God we need in every circumstance. Trust me; I know what I saw!

Better yet, trust Him!

Chapter 3

He Keeps His Stash Where?

First of all, I get that "the earth is the Lord's, and the fullness thereof" (Ps. 24:1, KJV), OK? I get that. So He does have a bank here! Yes, with all kinds of stocks and holdings: "the cattle upon a thousand hills" (Ps. 50:10, KJV). Impressive! But wait—there's more. What about the mouth of a fish that Jesus had Peter wrangle tax money out of (Matt. 17:27)? Not to mention "His riches in glory by Christ Jesus" (Phil. 4:19). Bottom line, He is loaded!

But every now and then—who am I kidding? more often than not, every day, all day!—God unearths some of His stash "to help in time of need" (Heb. 4:16). We recognize His activity and fondly refer to it as grace, unmerited favor, providence, intervention, mercy. Why not Insert Praise Here? His enduring love alone, His merciful kindness, which has been "great toward us" (Ps. 117:2), yea, "better than life" (Ps. 63:3), is more than enough reason to praise the Lord.

Don't stop now! Wait till you hear this anecdote—true story, coming out of the life of someone I know quite well, someone who benefited directly from God's hand in time of need. And I say "God's hand" because human intervention was untraceable in these events.

The summer of 1998 hovered closely on the heels of spring, especially for Eddison. That particular summer held great significance for him. A mere sophomore in these United States, he needed to register for one certain course that was only offered during the summer and that would propel him to seniority at the university where he was preparing for his master's degree.

Eddison was the sole provider for his young family of four. His wife, though a professional, took care of the home and of their two small daughters, ages six and four. It was a stretch indeed, for as the summer drew closer, needs crashed into each other with the relentlessness of reality. The girls needed new bikes; acquiring a washing machine was a major priority; the rent and other bills were due; he still had to feed his family; and if he were to forego this summer class, it would cost him a whole year, not to mention extra monies that he was unwilling and unable to shell out!

As he faced his needs and weighed them against his meager finances, Eddison found no humanly possible solution for his dilemma. He had exhausted all of those options some miles back, so to speak. There was no quick fix, no put-a-band-aid-over-it on this one! Eddison had no alternative but to take his plight directly to God.

He gathered his little family and decided to make this a matter of prayer for one whole week. He kept the promises of God ever in view and read daily quotations from the writings of Ellen G. White on praying in faith and putting God to the test. Eddison was steadfast in faith, encouraging his wife, who worried incessantly, partly because she was unemployed and could not contribute to a financial solution. But Eddison insisted that they trust God, bearing always in mind his favorite Bible text, which he still lives by today: "They that wait upon the Lord shall renew their strength; they shall mount up with wings as eagles; they shall run, and not be weary; and they shall walk, and not faint" (Isa. 40:31, KJV).

Days went by. Faith, God's promises, and consistent prayer, mixed in with a healthy dose of waiting on the Lord, were the weapons of choice when it came to their dilemma. When the seventh day came, God instructed Eddison to go to his bank and insert his bank card into the ATM. Eddison obeyed and went into the bank on that very day—Thursday. As he inserted his card and checked his balance, he found to his surprise that there was a deposit for $2,600 in his account! Not only did he have the $1,850 that he needed for the looming bills, including that crucial course, but there was a bonus of $750 after all was said and done!

Eddison went in to the bank officials to discuss the anonymous deposit in his account. They verified the authenticity of that deposit, stating that he was not mistaken, that no funds had been inadvertently misdirected into his account, but that if he wanted further proof, they would conduct an investigation into the matter and he would be informed by certified letter in seven to ten business days. Sure enough, their investigation confirmed what they had said to him on that eventful Thursday. The money was his to use, without fear or fault!

Eddison could hardly wait to go home to his family with the good news that Thursday. It was decidedly a moment of praise in their lives! For the benchmark of faith and the reward of promises fulfilled that they experienced that day, I dare say *Insert Praise Here!* God had done it again!

Yes, again! You see, two years earlier they had come to America to explore the possibility of moving here to study. It had been a faith move on their part, and when they had returned home to Tobago, they had found themselves without enough funds to restock their pantry and pay bills. Eddison had turned to his heavenly Father then, and as with the second instance, when he had gone into the bank, he had found a clear-cut deposit for $900, which the bank officials declared to be legitimately his funds; no mistake, no misdirection! In both cases he had no third party (at least of the human kind) on his account, nor was his account information privy to anyone outside of his bank. There was no gainsaying that in both cases Eddison's benefactor was God Himself.

What terrific interventions! What triumphs of faith! Again I shout, *Insert Praise Here!* How can we help but praise a God who cares for us in every way: a God who knows the very hairs of our head by number (and DNA coding), to whom we are "of more value than many sparrows" (Luke 12:7)? Yes, dear readers, God's supreme love and care for us are unquestionably guaranteed. He longs for us to prove Him, to take our situations to Him, to wait on Him for His providential intervention in His sovereign timing. If we would only relinquish control of our situations to Him, our God, who is by no means tight-fisted, but benevolent toward us in more ways than we can ask or think (Eph. 3:20), will "open [for us] the windows of heaven, and pour [us] out a blessing, that there shall not be room enough to receive it" (Mal. 3:10, KJV). Why not prove Him now in this?

Chapter 4

"Find 100 Ways ..."

Those who have tried it know full well that working full time and doing a full course load of study is no mean feat—not a sustainable undertaking by any means. I found that out when I decided to return to college while still teaching full time. What helped, if precious little, was the fact that the elementary school where I taught was on the campus of the college. I pushed through the best I could, often cutting into my lunch hour to take a much-needed class. As soon as the students were dismissed in the afternoon, I climbed the hill and made my way across campus to become the student for the next five or so hours after having been the teacher for some seven hours.

Needless to say, the time came when I could go on this way no longer. My graduation loomed ahead of me; courses crucial to my success were being scheduled during teaching time. It did not help that e-mail still wore diapers and MS-DOS had not been retired; online classes were hardly a figment of anyone's imagination at that juncture. I had to choose to take off one term (trimester) from teaching. Naturally, this meant that my salary would go into the pocket of the one who substituted for me. Having anticipated the lack of income, I had saved for this period.

Things went well for a while. But as with all good things, the money was coming to an end. I needed God's intervention on my behalf. Of course, I told Him so, because pray is what I do. I asked for God's help, claimed His promises, and waited (not necessarily patiently) for His direction. I didn't have much of a choice—I couldn't have returned to the job midstream; there was just too much to be done. Money went out, but none came in. Demand outweighed supply. What to do?

Those who know anything about God know that He delights in showing Himself strong (2 Chron. 16:9). Those who know Him a little better know that on occasion He likes to show Himself funny! Those are the times when you can't quite trace His direction, when "there is no searching of his understanding" (Isa. 40:28, KJV). That is, until you get it—and I did get it. Eventually.

Here's what happened: During one of the few—the very few—occasions when I actually went to chapel (assembly) at the college, God decided to show up with the answer to my prayers. Only I had no clue that He had actually orchestrated that particular chapel just for me! The main events of that assembly completely escape me—perhaps because, as with the earthquake, wind, and fire of Elijah fame (1 Kings 19:11, 12), God was not in any of those. Instead, He chose to cloak Himself in a sidebar, in one of the random announcements that boomed over the airwaves in spite of a more or less apathetic audience. The announcement said that as part of the seventieth-anniversary celebrations of the college, a special edition of the newsletter was to be circulated, and they were seeking ideas for a new name for the paper. The gauntlet was thrown. To sweeten the pot, the winning name would bring in $100.

Could it be? I thought as I left the assembly hall on my way to class. I had asked; could this be what was "given" me? I had been seeking; was this my "find"? Should I knock here? Would the door be "opened unto [me]" (Matt. 7:7, KJV)?

Excitement welled up in me. I thought, *Why not? What have I got to lose?* I thanked God for such an unexpected turn of events and solicited His help for a name. I stopped by the relevant office after my class and entered my name into the pool. Life went on as usual.

To my happy surprise, at the assembly that marked the close of the competition, it was announced that the winning name was the one I had submitted. I had won $100!

Earlier I stated that God shows Himself funny. The funny thing is that the $100 increase came at just the right time. I was on the brink of running on E, but God did not let me run out of gas.

Some might call it serendipity; others might surmise that it was just a fluke; but I say, *Insert Praise Here!* God had orchestrated it all along in His perfect will and providence. He did not leave me nor forsake me (Heb. 13:5); He had promised and did not deny Himself (2 Tim. 2:13).

God had proven Himself yet again, in all 100 ways at a time! What a precious experience that was, in spite of myself. What is even more precious is that God does not find just 100 ways. He has innumerable avenues by which to meet our need! He cares for us (1 Peter 5:7). He "shall supply all [our] need according to His riches in glory by Christ Jesus" (Phil. 4:19).

Let this knowledge provide you with assurance in God.

Chapter 5

Give Me the Runaround!

We are told in Hebrews 11:8 that it was by faith that "Abraham, when he was called to go out into a place which he should after receive for an inheritance, obeyed; and he went out, not knowing whither he went" (KJV). This speaks volumes about the level of implicit faith that Abraham exhibited in his God. In fact, the Bible boldly declares that "he staggered not at the promise of God through unbelief; but was strong in faith, giving glory to God" (Rom. 4:20, KJV). I dare say that Abraham had *Insert Praise Here!* moments—many more than I could list, were I to make this chapter all about him; however, dear reader, please take away from this introduction that Abraham had *faith*: faith enough to uproot his family without a clue as to where God was taking them. His motivation was that God said to get up, and he just did. Abraham *did not stagger* at God's promise, although it took close to 25 years before he actually saw its fulfillment. He kept the faith, *giving glory to God*—praising Him in advance—all 25 years during his wait, and during his entire life. God found these attitudes to be righteousness and counted them as such (Rom. 4:3).

We almost never have full disclosure with God; He reveals Himself and His plan in increments according to His timing, His providence; and He expects us to go along with the plan, whether or not all of our ducks are in a row. Sounds quite a bit like the runaround, does it?

In God's defense (yes, at this juncture, He needs one—sort of), it is Satan's job to dissuade us from believing that God is good. He runs interference with our faith and our hope in God, increases our angst, and stokes our desire to nuke our destiny like an instant meal rather than to have it develop its abundance of flavor—an abundance that Jesus Himself mentioned in John 10:10. On the other hand, what God has told us at the outset is that He has tremendous plans for us (Jer. 29:11), uppermost of which is our salvation (John 3:16; 2 Peter 3:9). Anything else, I guess, it is His prerogative to keep secret or to reveal to us at will (Deut. 29:29). Like Abraham, we might do well to put our faith to work and to obey (Heb. 11:8). Knowing where we're going is a plus; half the thrill is getting there ... or isn't that what someone once cleverly said?

A friend of mine once told me an amazing story about how he became a Seventh-day Adventist. It is, in my opinion, one of those situations where God gave someone the runaround. It all began—or it might be more correct to say that it came to his attention that God was actually doing this—when he was a young boy.

Kirk grew up in a Christian family. The family was very active in their denomination, and, as his recollection goes, church leaders saw potential in him even from an early age. They kept a close eye on young Kirk, taking him with them to conferences and various important meetings—grooming him, one might say.

There was always a yearning in Kirk's heart, one that was to be answered by God alone. While he appreciated the loving ministrations of his family and church leaders, the desire to close the gap between the God he knew and the God he wanted to know kept niggling at his insides. He had sensed very early that God had a hand on his life.

Just how much of a hand God had on Kirk's life could hardly be imagined, nor could the so-called runaround that accompanied God's hand. But then that afternoon came: the one where Kirk was walking along a street in New York City. All it took was a look down. Yes, a look down.

Kirk cast his eyes down on that particular day and saw the sheet of paper on the sidewalk. It happened to be a piece of Seventh-day Adventist literature. In an uncharacteristic move, even for him, Kirk picked up the tract and began reading it. Thus began his odyssey in this new faith.

At the back of the document was the address for the church from which the tract was issued. Kirk found the church and began attending in secret.

As stated before, Kirk was heavily entrenched in his other church. Switching to a new church could not have been the easiest decision to make. Perhaps this was why Kirk did not let others in on his discovery at first. In fact, neither his mother nor the rest of his family knew about his decision until they discovered that he was not on the job on Saturday but was actually attending church. He had been very clear with his boss that he could no longer work on Saturdays because he had begun to worship on the Sabbath.

Needless to say, his choice to pursue this uncharted path (in his family's view, at least) was met with misgivings; however, his faith in God and in his decision to follow Jesus in this manner grew and was strengthened. Kirk was baptized at the end of a series of meetings, and his mother was among the witnesses. As she observed her son in the weeks and months that followed, Kirk's mother noted the changes in her son's life, and she herself began attending his new church. Eventually she and some of his siblings were baptized into the Seventh-day Adventist Church.

When Kirk shared this story with me, I could hardly contain myself. I found it fascinating that God's runaround caused Kirk to look down in order to look up. I say, **Insert Praise Here!** because clearly God went out of the box on this one! Today Kirk is a strong believer with a unique and memorable ministry that encourages children in their walk with Jesus and inspires them to make choices that would lead them to the plans God has for their lives.

Stepping out on a runaround is hardly a comfortable activity for anyone to pursue. Take the apostle Paul. He was thrown from his horse, temporarily blinded, and set on a completely different path (Acts 9). A flipped switch, a classic runaround by any standard! As for my friend Kirk, life as he knew it was derailed by the simple act of looking down. He was diverted from well-groomed dreams and catapulted headlong into God's plan for his life. But he staggered not at his newfound faith, although it was born out of an unanticipated detour.

The lesson is, dear reader, that however unsettling a God-initiated runaround might be, it still holds that "the just shall live by faith: but if any man draw back, my soul shall have no pleasure in him," says God (Heb. 10:38, KJV). Sad truth is, "without faith it is impossible to please Him" (Heb. 11:6). Pleasing the One who gave His life so that we can have life and have it more abundantly (John 10:10) ought to unquestionably be our choice du jour—indeed, our choice *de la vie*, our utmost choice!

Chapter 6

Give Me the Runaround! II

We determined in the first runaround installment that God reveals Himself and His plan in increments according to His timing and His providence, and that He expects us to go along with the plan, as did Abraham, "not knowing whither he went" (Heb. 11:8, KJV). After all, God declared that "the just shall live by faith: but if any man draw back, my soul shall have no pleasure in him" (Heb. 10:38, KJV). For this reason—our desire to please God—if no other, we announce in response that "we are not of them who draw back unto perdition; but of them that believe to the saving of the soul" (Heb. 10:39, KJV).

God's runarounds have had their

effect on me as well. In the following two vignettes, God gives me orders that, like Abraham, I undertake to follow by faith, without knowing their outcomes.

In the first instance, God spoke to me while I was in traffic on my way home one afternoon. I should preface this by saying that God and I often spend quality time together during my commute. It is such a precious time. Much of what He says to me is said in the cab of that Jeep. He reveals Himself in my thoughts, and often I hear His sweet voice right there in my vehicle. How I treasure those moments! I could go on and on here about the sweetness of God's voice when we spend quality time together. Have you ever heard His voice? Please, I beg of you, *have* that experience, *long* for it, *pray* for it! It will change you in an indescribable way. I doubt my plug has done the experience of the voice of God justice, but that is just because my words fail me at this point. But I redeem myself and **Insert Praise Here!** for the voice of God.

At God's suggestion I always keep a stock of evangelistic literature in my car, within my reach. On this particular evening, God told me to grab a *Signs of the Times* and hand it through my window to someone in the traffic. *Oh, yes? Who, Lord?* I asked, debating whether it was the man on the motorcycle or the one in the black van, or the person in the white T-shirt ...

As I deliberated over the prospects, the light turned green and the moment was lost. I felt as if I had let God down and apologized repeatedly, promising God that the next time I slowed down, I would give the magazine to whoever was on hand.

I turned onto the service road to skirt the traffic. As I detoured onto another side street, I saw two men standing on the side of the road. Very unceremoniously I put the window down, slowed as I approached them, and stuck my arm out the window with the magazine at the end of it. "Excuse me," I said to both men, "I just wanted you to have this." Then I stepped on the gas. Unfortunately, my car did not cooperate with me to move fast enough up the hill, for although the gentlemen received the magazine out of my hand, as soon as they read the title, they threw it onto the roof of my car.

Sadness crept over me as I kept driving and the *Signs of the Times* fell off my car into the street behind me. I said to myself as much as to God, "If they only knew ..." If they only knew what God could do in their lives, that all the answers lay at His feet, that what came to them on the pages of that magazine could determine their eternal destiny ... If only they could grasp that God had visited them on that afternoon, making His grace appear to them (Titus 2:11)!

I drove home and prayed for them during my evening worship time. I prayed that at least one of the men would change his mind and return for the magazine. The next day I made it my business to take the same route on the way home. I was heartened to find that the magazine was nowhere to be found. From what I could see, it had not blown to the side of the street. Nor did I think that it had made the garbage. Rather, I chose to believe that it was retrieved by one or both men, or that someone else saw the treasure in the middle of the street, as my friend Kirk did, and retrieved it. I began to praise God immediately, and God reminded me that His Word would never return to Him void (Isa. 55:11). In fact, God pointed out that it would either convert or convict; that His Word either saves those who choose to be saved or condemns those who choose otherwise; that it either bears witness *for* those who believe in Him or bears witness *against* those who deny Him. Either way, His Word would accomplish its purpose, God assured me.

At sharing time in staff worship shortly thereafter, I related this experience and the conclusion that God had revealed to me about this event. I seized the opportunity to encourage my colleagues to keep these unknown men in prayer. Who knew what this magazine would do, where it would reach? One can only imagine, I intimated.

While this God-given runaround has not had its conclusion revealed to me at this date, I still say, **Insert Praise Here!** because God chose me as the catalyst to begin what might have far-reaching effects even when I move on. Some things God may choose to reveal only in heaven, and as Sovereign, that is His prerogative, His alone!

In another instance that happened years before, God decided to take me on what I fondly refer to as an escapade. It was during the time of the launching of a book on the Ten Commandments. I took a few of them to keep in my car and to distribute at will, but God had other plans for those books.

I had the unmitigated gall to pray to God that He would show me who should receive those books out of my hand. He decided to answer my prayer in a way that I would have hardly expected. I suppose in hindsight that He desired my bold prayer so that I would acknowledge my willingness to be used by God and so that God could entrust me with such a mission.

Having been satisfactorily reassured that I was game, God told me to go first to a very popular church in the suburbs. I was to address the book to its pastor and to leave it in a location that He would show me. (Sound familiar? Like Abraham's call on its side, somewhat?) Anyway, I did as I was told and visited the church. During the pastor's sermon, I felt as if I was sitting on pins and needles, keyed up with curiosity. *Where, Lord, where?* Eventually God showed me the exact spot where I was to leave the book. After I did the deed, I walked into the sunlit afternoon, feeling a rush of pleasure at having been an undercover agent for God. I was excited, fully on board with the plan, so much so that I prayed all week for its success and expressed great anticipation for the next assignment.

For the next five Sundays and on one Wednesday night, God answered my question: Where to, Lord? I attended masses, prayer meetings, and various church services, each time delivering God's package in the place assigned—a place I knew only at the time of delivery. The adrenaline rush was heady, but what was most appealing in this entire mission was that someone, *someone*, was going to find those books. They would read them or maybe even throw them out for someone else to find, and the Holy Spirit would gain access. The exponential potential of this covert operation was too fascinating, even for me!

I kept this under wraps for a while, letting only one other person in: my mother, a prayer warrior whose prayers followed me as I went out, not knowing whither I went. I may never find out the extent of these particular runaround episodes on this side of heaven; let God have His private joy spree now. But just to have been elected as a participant in the Great Commission in such a fashion leaves me no choice but to *Insert Praise Here!* As God promised, He was with me always (Matt. 28:20) and I did receive power from the Holy Spirit (Acts 1:8) as I made myself available for God's call to be a witness for Him. I thank Him ever so often for having been granted such an opportunity.

I could have chosen to view this runaround in quite a different way. I could, like Jonah, have argued with God about the path He had chosen; the uncertainty; in my case, the risk of being caught; the seeming futility of it all. This would have

41

played right into Satan's scheme. That's right: Satan would have us believe that God is out to manipulate us, to bend us according to His own will, to brainwash us into believing that He is justified in giving us the runaround and that we are getting the short end of the stick.

Nothing could be further from the truth. For when we consider what Jesus gave up for us, the wounds He bore in His person, the bruises He bore for our iniquities, those stripes of His through which we are healed from sin (Isa. 53:5), the restoration which His sacrifice has wrought—yea, our salvation—we are compelled by His great love for us to surrender our lives, our wills to Him. We are compelled to take up His yoke (Matt. 11:29), runaround and all, and to bear witness of His goodness (Ps. 136:1; 100:5), letting others know the truth about Him (John 10:10). We can trust Him, knowing that all things will work together for our good (Rom. 8:28), even when God gives us the runaround!

Chapter 7

"Something Happened to Daddy"

Yes, well ... something did happen—long before he was ever my daddy. It happened before he met and married my mother. In fact, it all began, as he would tell it, when he was but a youngster. I have a feeling, though, that this thing had been orchestrated long before he was born (Ps. 139:16), if God had anything to do with it—which, naturally, He did!

This is the way Daddy tells it:

"My father and mother were Anglicans, so I was born into an Anglican family; sent to the Delaford [East Tobago] Anglican

School, known then as the St. Paul's E. C. School; and taught the Anglican catechism, which included the Ten Commandments, during the morning sessions. In the afternoon sessions the teachers taught that the first of the week was Sunday and the seventh day was Saturday.

"I was only about five years old, but I was puzzled. I could not understand how Sunday, the first day of the week, was church day, and Saturday, the seventh day, was treated as an ordinary workday. So at home I repeated aloud, 'The days of the week are Monday, Tuesday, Wednesday, Thursday, Friday, Saturday, Sunday.' My father told me that Sunday was indeed the first day and Saturday the seventh.

"'How come people go to church on Sundays and not on Saturdays?' I asked.

"'Because Jesus was resurrected on the first day of the week; the Sabbath was changed from Saturday to Sunday,' he replied. The answer satisfied me then.

"In the latter half of the 1940s Pastor G. Ralph Thompson [who later served as secretary of the General Conference of

Seventh-day Adventists] held a crusade in Delaford, which created no mean stir in my little village. I was not taken to or allowed to attend any of the meetings, but children who attended did give an excellent report about them in school, and I was thrilled by what I heard. The villagers loved Pastor Thompson's preaching. It was spoken about in the rum shops [bars/public houses], groceries, schools, everywhere. This prompted the Anglican minister, Rev. Jacobs, to have us children repeat after him, 'A Seventh-day Adventist is not a Christian; a Seventh-day Adventist is a Jew.'

"Later in that decade—in fact, in 1949—an SDA family became our neighbors. They lent me the book *The Hope of the Race*. I was intrigued by what I read. I was also introduced to the Junior Voice of Prophecy Bible Course, the Twentieth Century Bible Course, and the Faith Bible Course. Then around 1955 Pastor Edison S. Pascall held a series of meetings in the village. This time I attended and wanted to be baptized, but my father resisted. Unfortunately, Pastor

Pascall drowned at Roxborough Bay during the last week of the meetings. It was a most traumatic experience for every villager.

"I don't know what happened, but in the years that followed I became a party animal, a drinker, and a smoker, and I committed gross sins. I did not have time for God. I stopped praying. My life was in shambles. But God never stopped pursuing me. He would speak to me in the parties and during the Carnivals [a major holiday in Trinidad and Tobago, equivalent to Mardi Gras], and sometimes in order to crowd out His voice from my consciousness, I would drink more alcohol.

"Then everything began to lose the excitement: the music, parties, fetes; but I was hooked on alcohol and tobacco.

"One night while in a drunken state, on my way home, an overwhelming desire for deliverance came over me. I was unhappy with my condition. I wanted, needed deliverance! I made sure that no one was looking at me, and then I knelt down in the middle of the tract of road and prayed. I cried unto God for help, and He heard my cry. I was delivered.

"However, I could not stay in the Delaford environment, so I went to Caribbean Union College, now the University of the Southern Caribbean [in Trinidad], where I fully accepted the Lord Jesus Christ and was baptized by Pastor G. Ralph Thompson [the very pastor who had held meetings in my village 15 years prior] on February 29, 1964.

"I know that the Lord hears the sincere prayers of even drunkards, because He heard me."

So, yes, something *did* happen to Daddy. God reached in and snatched him out of the devil's grip. And the way he tells it, when he got up from his knees that evening in the middle of the road, he knew he was delivered because the desire for alcohol and tobacco was completely removed from his mind and his system. In fact, he was so repulsed by them thereafter that he has never touched a drop nor has he lit up since that evening of victory. And I say, *Insert Praise Here!* because God has proved Himself in my father's life—proved that "He is also able to save to the uttermost those who come to God through Him, since He always lives to make intercession for them" (Heb. 7:25, NKJV).

Is your life in shambles? Are you or someone you know at the end of your rope? Do you think it's all over, that you've done your worst, and that there is just no way out? If it didn't take the first time, read this story again. Let yourself admit the truth that God pursues you all through your life, despite the turns that you might take. He loves you and wants to save you (John 3:16). He wants to fix it all for you; won't you let Him? "Something happened to Daddy"; it can happen to you, too!

Chapter 8

God Said, "Yes—And I Mean It!"

No ... ! What? Give up our friends, our beloved "Grande" Church? We're what? WHAT?! This was not the way I had envisioned the end of that particular Communion service. Yes, the elder had announced that there would be a meeting of all the members from the Coal Mine-Jairasingh region on his left, our right, immediately after the benediction. The brethren had congregated in the designated spot. Naturally, my siblings and I had taken our seats among the assembly, for we were villagers from that region.

The pastor addressed us. He expressed his pleasure at the thought of our establishment of a company that would meet in our village starting the next Sabbath—*no*—and announced that my father, who was first elder of the Sangre Grande Church that year, would become the first elder of the Coal Mine Company—*No*—and that my mother would be the Sabbath school superintendent—*NO!*

No, this can't be happening! I said to myself. We were going to have to leave our friends. There were few, very few children among those of us from Coal Mine Village: my older sister; I, the middle child; my brother, who was a year younger than I; a couple of other children who were a few years younger than we were; and maybe one older—that was it! We had our lifelong friends in Grande Church. What were we to do without them?

The amens from the adults echoed around us. They were overjoyed that their dream was coming true. How well I remembered the late Sister Adella Hoyte bringing up the idea of a church in Coal Mine Village any number of times when the prayer cell convened at her house. She had even offered the use of her "downstairs" for that purpose. True, her husband had used it for his upholstery workshop, but we could use one half of it—why not? *NO!!!*

As the conversation swirled around us, we realized that the adults' dream was our nightmare. We were going to be unceremoniously torn away from our friends, we learned, and would not see them until the twelfth Sabbath, when we would return to Grande Church for the Communion service, and on those rare occasions when there would be a special program at the "mother church," as the Sangre Grande Church would henceforth be known to us. *No!!!*

Not only were we going to be separated from our friends; removed from our beloved Sabbath school class; and deprived of the wonderful choirs, the organ, the piano, and the fine way in which we worshipped; we were now going to meet under someone's house, in a "building" with no walls, no floor, and no musical instruments! Our

51

Sabbath school props would consist of one set of felts that the mother church had spared, and our children's Sabbath school would meet in the "room" also designated as the vestry. *What?! NO!!*

Yes. God had said yes, yes to that idea. Our protestations were like white noise to Him. He had a plan, and it was a go.

It was finally decided that our next-door neighbors, the Horrells, would let us use their downstairs for the church. It had been their idea to build it up so that one of their daughters and her family could live there, but since construction was not underway at that time, why not use it for the time being? No problem. No? YES. Completely yes.

The important details satisfactorily sorted out, the assembly put it to a vote; the vote was carried, to their breathless joy; and we were prayed out. Needless to say, the ride home that Sabbath afternoon was heavy-hearted. Our driver was informed of the changes to the Sabbath arrangement. Why would we need his services when to step out of our gate now meant heading into the church? Well, except on the twelfth Sabbath, of course, or when the mother church had a special event.

I remember the week of preparation that followed. The Horrells demolished the croton hedge that outlined the front of their yard. The ground foliage was also removed, and gravel and a thin slab of concrete were put in its place. Two rows of foundation bricks were lined up to create the steps at the entrance of the "church." The down-stairs was cleared of any and all debris that it housed so that it could now house the presence of God. A metal sheet gate, oth-erwise known as "galvanize," was placed at the entrance and held up by a couple more foundation bricks. A plywood wall was erected to house the vestry-cum-children's Sabbath school; the rest of the plywood was used to build the rostrum.

On Thursday or Friday afternoon—which one, I forget—a white lorry [truck] pulled up, and some church men depos-ited the "crusade benches" that would be used for pews, as well as a few chil-dren's benches for the children's room; a borrowed crusade amplifier, speaker, and microphone; and an old crusade pulpit. A vintage lobby table with carved legs belonging to the Horrells, a doily, and our dining room table arrangement, which we would take to the church each Sabbath morning, rounded out the assortment of furnishings, fixtures, and fittings that graced the Coal Mine Company's sanctuary. Oh, did I mention that the electricity came from upstairs via an extension cord that ran through a hole in the floor? That was as real as it got, folks!

Despite our ardent prayers to the contrary, on June 6, 1981, our church congregated for its opening service in Coal Mine Village, "under Mom's house." What made it worse, at least in our estimation, was that my sister and I were automatically designated church janitors! We were to ensure that the church was swept clean and that the benches were wiped of any dust, both on Friday in preparation for the Sabbath and on Sunday afternoon for the Sunday night meetings.

We were not going to have our way on

this one, we finally conceded, so we were determined to make the best of it. What was nice, though, was that among our charter members that first Sabbath were a 19-year-old woman who had backslidden from the mother church and a young man, "Mom's" nephew, who had grown up around Adventism but had never joined. They had met during the young woman's time away from church and were living together. Through prayer and concerted effort, the young woman and the man had decided to be baptized. The Thursday prior to the church's opening, a church brother with land donated a lot opposite his own house, and members came together to build the couple a house in one day. Yes! On that Friday afternoon, which happened to be my birthday, they were married and baptized in the mother church. They came to us a baptized, married couple, ready to participate in building up the Coal Mine Company. Yes! The young woman could sing and had been a former Sabbath school secretary at the Sangre Grande Church; the young man was a musician and had his own acoustic guitar, which he brought to church that very first Sabbath. Having grown up around Adventism, he was familiar with many of the hymns. What he didn't know he picked up readily, being the quick study that he was.

That young couple became stalwarts in the congregation. The young man became an elder, an AY leader, and one of the most fantastic Sabbath school teachers we ever had. He continued to provide music, bringing in a synthesizer keyboard when keyboards came out. We later formed a band: he on lead or acoustic guitar; my brother also on acoustic, which he sometimes played as lead, main, or bass; and I on his Casio keyboard. His wife became one of the Sabbath school superintendents, church chorister, and a favored "singer in Israel." She, my sister, and I formed a singing trio, later named Para Cristo, which sang together for many years until my sister went off to college.

As a company we learned how to do church. We became a well-oiled machine, not missing a beat in terms of church operations. We also became a cohesive unit. Everyone supported each other and was encouraged to participate in the work of the Lord. Not incredibly, the generation gap was for the most part narrowed, if not closed.

All was not smooth sailing, though. A number of the villagers who lived opposite or adjacent visited on occasion but did not commit. In fact, some never came at all. Even worse, there was an extremely tall palm tree between the church and our closest neighbor. That palm tree was the "liming spot" (neighborhood hangout) for most of the young men from the area. They would hang out and be rowdy at times but tended to disperse when it was time for the preached word.

Worse yet, the neighbors directly opposite eventually decided to reopen the once thriving "parlor" (neighborhood corner store/dry goods establishment) that had been closed for years after the deaths of the proprietors, their grandparents. Only this time they turned it into a rum shop (public house/bar). They would throw open the doors on Sabbath morning, roll out and hook up the speakers, and blast calypso music during our services. During cricket season they would blare the broadcasts, which sadly skewed our attention levels. It was their intention to drown out the voice of the Holy Spirit, and to a great degree they succeeded. Many of the young men so abused their bodies with alcohol, tobacco, and marijuana and lived such aimless lives that many of them died in their thirties and forties with nothing to show for themselves. It was sad, and I often wondered how they were able to live such useless lives. I shake my head even now. Why could we not have reached them? It was the saddest thing to me, to us.

The Holy Spirit did not stop, however. He instructed us to move into the outlying areas. We went back to areas we had previously evangelized, even before the church was established, and held evangelistic meetings, at one time under the same house where I had made my decision for God a few years earlier. One gentleman, known in the village as "Tarzan," attended the meetings with his family, as he had done during the year of my baptism. He was moved by the words he heard, but, sadly, when decision time came, he was not among the persons who were baptized. However, the church's ranks grew by a few.

We continued to spread our evangelistic tentacles, going into the northern, southern, eastern, and western areas of our village. We gave Bible studies, held sunshine bands, hosted Vacation Bible Schools, did street ministries, conducted Harvest Ingathering campaigns, distributed literature, and continued to hold crusades and revivals. Our membership grew from the twenties to the forties to the sixties—and finally it even surpassed the hundred mark. Among the new recruits was a large contingent of youth. We were no longer alone; we had *friends*! Yes! Together we learned how to be the type of people God wanted us to be. We had some great leaders with a heart for the youth. They knew just what to do with us, about us, for us. We formed a nucleus that was hard to crack even when we had occasion to attend the mother church.

Hmm ...

People from other churches came to visit us and never left. One particular family came to visit one Sabbath. The wife had recently returned to the Adventist faith; the husband accompanied his wife to church but was not a convert. They had just moved to the northernmost end of the village and were looking for a church to call home. The children were impressed by the fact that the service was not as long as the mother church's, which they had visited the week before. They returned the next Sabbath and have never left to this day. The father was eventually baptized and became one of the stalwart elders and a most efficient church treasurer, Sabbath school teacher, and AY leader. His wife became a mother in Israel; a superintendent; a director of music, education, and family life. The children learned from the ground up, as did I. Yes!

The church eventually outgrew its meager accommodations. By the help of God, we acquired a piece of property on a hill, where the current church building stands today. The building was dedicated;

we were installed as charter members of a fully formed church, whose ranks continue to swell, even today; and later we became a lead church in a new district that was established. We were weaned from our mother. Yes on that one, too—from God and, without hesitation, from me!

On that note I say, *Insert Praise Here!* You see, God always had all of these things in mind (Jer. 29:11), and so many more that this chapter could hardly do justice to. While I in my myopic state screamed NO, God said yes and insisted yes: Yes to the fact that I would grow up in a tight-knit, caring, loving congregation and as a result would never give in to the pull of the world, even as a youth. I dare say that God plopped me into that congregation knowing full well that it would be my mainstay, my place where I would grow with Him so much that to this day I know nothing else but a relationship with Him; that even now when I am severely tried, I can conclude without fail that God alone makes sense. Yes on that as well.

I repeat, *Insert Praise Here!* For many a

pastoral intern's ministry was honed on the backs of the "Coal Miners." Among those interns my brother-in-law stands out—*Yes! A million times yes!* My sister would gladly affirm this. Aside from those who were imported, Coal Mine SDA Church itself has produced a handful of pastors from within its ranks, a number of teachers, college professors, musicians, chefs, civil servants, and gainfully employed workers of all kinds, many of whom are employed in some direct or indirect way in the cause of God—another *YES!!!* The youth of my time have grown up; some have married and started families; some have moved away; but many remain to carry on the work of the Lord in Coal Mine. Yes!

What tickles me is that, though they did not sprout when first planted, some seeds have germinated twenty or thirty years later. Two quick stories: my mother and I gave a series of Bible studies to a young woman in Jairasingh Village (a village bordering Coal Mine). She believed but was not fully persuaded. She never made the decision for Christ. Fast-forward some twenty years: I received the glad news that her son, who was a babe in diapers at the time of our encounters, was now a full-fledged baptized member of the Coal Mine SDA Church and actively involved in the communications department, among other things. YES!!! And what of "Tarzan"? Well, as of 2011, he was baptized into the church—some thirty-odd years later. *YES!!!* And, believe it or not, the half has not been told, the end is not yet—all fitting clichés that well characterize the ongoing saga of the Coal Mine Seventh-day Adventist Church. Yes, *yes,* and YES!!!

We said no; God said yes. Who knew best? God, that's who! He knew all along that all these things would transpire. He knew that the salvation of all these people—and our salvation, too—hung on the establishment of His house in that part of His vineyard. He wanted us to make Him a sanctuary that He might dwell among us (Exod. 25:8). He wanted to dwell among *us,* in *our* village; was there a no on that? No. Yes on that! Yes to that; yes to God!

So what is the conclusion of the whole

matter? God, who is the King eternal, immortal, invisible, the only wise God (1 Tim. 1:17), has all the answers—all of them! When He says yes, it's a yes! At times we would prefer His yes to be a no, and at other times we would give anything for His no to be a yes. But God knows all things and gives His answers in His own perfect way, according to His own perfect will.

One insightful lyricist, Babbie Mason, sums it up this way:

God is too wise to be mistaken;
God is too good to be unkind.
So when you don't understand,
When you don't see His plan,
When you can't trace His hand,
Trust His heart.
That would be a YES!!!

***

Subsequent to the writing of this chapter, toward the close of 2011, I received a fascinating news item from my mother. That very Sunday morning at around 10:00 there would be a soil-turning for a television studio on land adjoining the property of the Coal Mine SDA Church. The land belonged to a Seventh-day Adventist attorney. He had purchased it with the intention of moving to Coal Mine. However, the land sat there unused. It seems that God had other intentions for it.

A young SDA pastor who listened to the call of God to extend his level of ministry began an Internet radio station called Resurface Radio. It currently broadcasts out of a small studio at the headquarters of the South Caribbean Conference of Seventh-day Adventists in St. Augustine, Trinidad. As my mother told it, the pastor's dream included branching out into television ministry. The attorney, who also happens to host one of the programs on Resurface Radio, willingly donated his land—the very land adjacent to the Coal Mine Church's property—toward the building of a television station/studio.

My mother added that already the congregation is aware of persons who might be pivotal in the broadcasts that will be produced out of this television station. She mentioned the wife of a young man who has been associated with the Coal Mine Church from his childhood but who has never been baptized. His uncle is the current first elder of the church; consequently, this young man attended the Adventist elementary school in Sangre Grande and has held membership in Sabbath school classes at Coal Mine. In his adulthood he met and married a young woman who started attending church with the family. She is now a baptized member of the Coal Mine Church. According to my mother and other members of the church, this young lady is naturally gifted as a communicator and is already slated in their minds as a potential anchor for the television station. My mother and I marveled together on that November morning at God's work revealed—marveled that He had established Coal Mine Church with such wonderful sequels in mind. He trained us to run like a well-oiled machine because He knew that such an endeavor would be placed in the mind of Pastor Courtney Francois, that Elder Dale Scobie would say yes when God asked for his land, that the young Mrs. Morris would be a natural for such an endeavor, and that Coal Mine Church itself would rally around such vision and ministry.

I decided awhile ago that God does nothing in a vacuum. He "doeth all things well," the late hymnist Fanny Jane Crosby once wrote of Jesus. Undoubtedly I must *Insert Praise Here!*

Chapter 9

God Said, "No—HEY!"

I had always wanted to go to Antigua. In fact, I was determined to live and work there after my graduation from college. You can imagine my excitement when I learned that recruiters from the North Caribbean Conference of Seventh-day Adventists, of which Antigua was a part, were on campus that week, and that there were vacancies for teachers in that conference.

At my first opportunity, I spoke to the powers that be. I interviewed favorably with the president of that conference himself, along with other dignitaries. They informed me of the channels I needed to pursue in order to make my dream a reality. I followed the prescribed protocol, composing my cover letter and curriculum vitae and stating my interest in being employed at one of their elementary schools, with Antigua as my preference. I got the preferred number of character references and with confidence put my package together. I sent it off with a prayer of thanksgiving on my lips, having secured the assurance from the officials that I would hear from them within the next few weeks, as they were anxious to fill the vacancies.

Recruiters from the East Caribbean Conference (which at the time included Barbados, St. Vincent and the Grenadines, St. Lucia, and Dominica) and my own South Caribbean Conference were also on hand, and our deans and counselors had advised us to speak to them all. I therefore placed applications with all of them, as well as with the Ministry of Education of the government of Trinidad and Tobago. As a first-time formal applicant for a teaching job, I knew it was reasonable to do so.

I graduated in memorable fashion and did the necessary licentiate examinations to deem me a fit instructor according to the laws of Trinidad and Tobago. Then the waiting game began.

I kept myself occupied during those summer months—with what, I can't fully remember. However, my prayers ascended faithfully, and my dream grew greater within me, along with my sense of adventure. From a very young age I had wanted to become a missionary. I had dreams of travelling to various countries of the world, of working for Christ in various areas of His vineyard. Such was the Adventist jargon I had grown up hearing, which had helped to nurture the seed of mission adventure that had taken root within my soul. First stop, Antigua!

July dragged on, but not before taking the electricity and the water supply with it. It was not because we had failed to pay the utility bills; it was typical of village living at that time. Impatiently we carried on while the electric and water companies took their own sweet time to fulfill their promises to repair their respective utilities. Shortly after the power came back on, the telephone service was cut. Again we were current with our bills, but, as usual, the utility companies were substandard.

That was when my nerves really kicked in. Any day now I was expecting a phone call from the North Caribbean Conference to inform me of my placement. I prayed earnestly about this dilemma, claiming every relevant promise in the Bible and thanking God that whatever I asked in His name He was going to do (John 14:14).

I believed that God had said yes, but the truth of the matter was that God had said no. HEY! No? God would say no to my desire to work for Him as a missionary, in one of His schools? Really?

OK, let me clarify: God did say yes to my desire, but to the where of it He said no. Before your puzzled frown becomes permanent, let me explain. August came and went, and to my dismay the telephone service was not restored that whole time! While my angst built and my faith was tested and I made my disappointment known to God, He presented me with an alternative opportunity to teach at my alma mater, the Sangre Grande SDA School. Not only was my father was still teaching there, but it was one of the prime Adventist schools in Trinidad and Tobago, and it was government-assisted, meaning that while it was thoroughly parochial in nature, the government was responsible for the salary of the teachers. In other words, we would be paid as if we were teaching in a government school while practicing our teaching according to SDA standards!

Not at all surprisingly, I took the position. One might think it would have been odd to have some of my former teachers and my own father as colleagues, but it wasn't at all. Everyone was thoroughly professional, and, rather than hover, they let me be, encouraging where necessary and mentoring in all the right places. I was able to develop my craft and serve God first "in Jerusalem" (Acts 1:8). That must have been the masterful plan of God, because when I got home after my first evening of teaching, my mother informed me that the telephone service had been restored after six long weeks. What's more, the North Caribbean Conference Education Department had called. They had been calling for weeks on end trying to get a hold of me. When I returned their call that very day, I found out that they had great news for me: I was approved to work in one of the elementary schools in Antigua, and my position was still open. Was I still interested in it, as they still were in me?

It pained my heart to turn them down, but how could I do otherwise after having signed the employment contract locally and completing one full day of work? It was unthinkable to bail on my new responsibilities, even though what I had dreamed of all along was now in my hand, albeit one day late because of the incompetence of the telephone company!

I went to work the next day with mixed sentiments. I was happy to have a job but saddened by what I felt I had lost. But I kept hearing my mother's voice reminding me that "all things work together for good to them that love God, to them who are the called according to his purpose" (Rom. 8:28, KJV). I had to accept it: God had said no to Antigua.

I worked at my alma mater for four un-interrupted years. When I decided to return to college to continue my studies, God opened up a way for me in a fantastic fashion that only bespeaks His providential flair. It happened that a pastor was relocating to one of the districts in the Sangre Grande region. His wife taught at the elementary school on the college campus. She needed a job in Sangre Grande; I needed a job in Maracas. God orchestrated the switcheroo! In keeping with His Acts 1:8 odyssey for me, I now consider this my "Judea." The bonus was that my salary was not affected, since the Maracas SDA School was also government-assisted.

I did another four years of ministry at the elementary school on the college campus. After my graduation I needed to move out of the college area. True to form, God did the switcheroo again: same persons, same schools! The pastor was transferred back to the northwestern region of Trinidad, and his wife needed to move. I was happy to be back in my hometown!

I stayed at the Sangre Grande SDA School for one more year. The following year I was hired by an SDA principal of a non-denominational school to teach first grade in the United States. I suppose this had to be my "Samaria," if Acts 1:8 still applied. Two years later an opportunity presented itself (courtesy of God, I say with full assurance!) for me to once again be a part of the Seventh-day Adventist education system, this time in the North American Division. I accepted the call and have been here ever since. My "uttermost part of the earth" (KJV)? That is yet to be determined. For the time being, I must joyfully *Insert Praise Here!* For what I could not see at the time was this path through which God was bringing me to an "expected end" (Jer. 29:11, KJV)—well, unexpected, by my estimation! Notwithstanding, God has grown me and has done some of His finest work in me during these past few years. He has expanded my ability to minister and has given me a platform upon which to base my integration of faith and learning. That platform basically asserts:

God is real and can be trusted.

God can visit you, call you at any time, and reveal Himself to you—He did call Samuel when he was very young!

You don't have to wait until you grow up to be what Jesus wants you to be.

It was during this period that I was commissioned to the teaching ministry, and God has opened doors for me to be of wider service, even to the teachers of the conference and the union under which I serve. It was also during this time that I began to have a better sense of the presence of God in my personal space, to the point where, for example, only this year I was able to experience Him knocking on the window of my car and joining me for the rest of the ride home. I have always had a relationship with God, but that particular day was special because I was actually able to experience Him wanting to spend time with me, just because …

When I think of all the blessings and favor that God has extended toward me in spite of myself, I cannot help but *Insert Praise Here!* While I have no definitive reason for His decision, nor have I been made aware of any evidence that my going to Antigua would have been a misstep, I simply thank Him for this Ebenezer (1 Sam. 7:12). Many may offer their noble speculations, rendering the whole Antigua thing (or lack thereof) one of those events that "happen for a reason," while others might dare to suggest that, had I gone there, I might have experienced some sort of misfortune. I prefer not to waste my time on mere speculation. Ultimately, only God knows the real story, and in His sovereign authority, His answer to that particular prayer was no.

If there is anything to be taken away from this, dear readers, it is that God is still the reliable life coach, the only one who really sees all and knows all. While it may not appear so at the time, His "no" is not a bad thing—not at all! He does not leave us hanging, even when He says no. He promises that He is much more willing to give *good things* to those who ask Him than any parent is to give to his or her children (Matt. 7:11). In the end, God has only our best interest at heart, and if we exercise our faith and let Him, He will show Himself strong (2 Chron. 16:9) and work all things for our good (Rom. 8:28).

It's just a matter of time …

Chapter 10

God Said, "Wait—How Great is Your Faith?"

The good news was that I was going to have 13 students in my first grade that year. The bad news was that Angela was not coming back. Angela not coming? I had waited all year to have her in class. Her sister Anita had been my student the previous year, and she was so precious. In fact, all three sisters—Arita, Angela, and Anita Santos—were among the sweetest students a teacher could ask for. Why was this happening?

The principal sadly explained that both parents were struggling financially. The father had lost his job, and the mother was barely out of college. They were unable to make ends meet and keep all three girls in an Adventist school. As much as they believed in Seventh-day Adventist Christian education, they had no other recourse, given their situation, but to enroll their children in public school.

Public school? There was no way that these sweet little girls would survive in public school! They just were not wired for that. Besides, their parents believed in the mandate that "all thy children shall be taught of the Lord, and great shall be the peace of thy children" (Isa. 54:13, KJV). It broke their hearts to have to do what was to them the unthinkable—to go against that very mandate.

Public school? I would not hear of it; I could not hear of it! I turned to God—perhaps turned *on* Him might be a tad more accurate. "Lord, you *promised* that all Your children shall be taught of the Lord,"

I accused. "*You* said that when it comes to Your will, if we ask *anything*, we will receive it [Matt. 7:7; 21:22; John 16:24; 1 John 5:14, 15]. Now here are these Santos girls. *You* made them; You *know* that they are unable to survive in public school. They are *Your* children; they belong in *Your* school. No, *no!* I am not going to accept this," I blazed. "You said that Your eyes run to and fro throughout the whole earth to show yourself strong on behalf of those whose heart is loyal to You [2 Chron. 16:9]. No, no, Lord: You are *not* going to get off on this one—no way! *You* promised. This is Your opportunity to do just that: to show Yourself strong. On *Your* word: *You* fix it!"

I walked out of my room and sought the teachers who were to have Arita and Anita that year. They sadly informed me of the girls' departure, not sure that I had heard of it. We agreed that they could not survive in public school and shook our heads in pity. However, I did not let God off the hook. I said to those teachers that this was not over, that God *had* to do something—He just had to. *Hmm,* they responded.

I found the vice principal, and we had a similar conversation, only this time I added that I believed that God was going to work it out; that, in fact, I *was* going to have Angela in my class that year despite the present outlook. "I told God—I *told* Him—that He is going to have to prove Himself," I said to the vice principal. "After all, He has instructed me to teach my students that He is real and can be trusted. What better way for Him to provide proof of His reality and trustworthiness than to show up in this situation?"

The vice principal was earnest. She shared with me another story in which God had provided for another student, and she immediately set out to see what we could do as a staff to help the Santos family. We prayed together, agreeing on God's intervention in this matter (Matt. 18:19, 20), and I returned to prepare my classroom for the upcoming school year. The gauntlet had been thrown; it was now on God to do something about this situation.

Later one of the assistant teachers came into my classroom and offered to help me write the names of my students in their books. I asked her to prepare a set for Angela.

"Angela?" she asked incredulously.

"Yes, Angela," I replied.

"You know they aren't coming back?" she queried.

"God will do it," I replied calmly.

"O ... K," the assistant said, resignedly shrugging her shoulders. She cocked her head to one side and proceeded to label the workbooks with the blue permanent marker I had provided for her.

I stuck Angela's name tag to her desk, set her books inside, and made her a first-day-of-school welcome packet as I always did for each student. At the teachers' assembly, I made known to the teachers what I had done. After all, I *was* going to have Angela in my class that year.

The staff looked at me. The principal had announced prior to my declarations that we should pray for the Santos family.

"They *are* going to come back," I insisted. "God promised. He wants His children to be educated in His school. And I have learned that when it comes to God's direct will, when we put it before Him, He has no recourse but to work it out, because He cannot deny Himself [2 Tim. 2:13]."

So we made it a matter of prayer. We prayed at that assembly and at many others to follow. I never ceased to flash this issue before God's face. "Continuing instant in prayer" is how I think He Himself referred to it in the Bible (Rom. 12:12, KJV). That's what I did. I walked over to her desk, sat in her seat, laid hands on her desk, walked up and down my classroom, and interceded with God on behalf of my beloved Angela and her sisters, citing the infallibility of God's Word every time and thanking Him that He was going to show this teacher and the rest of the staff at His school that He cared and that His Word was real.

The first day of school arrived, and the Santos girls were nowhere in sight. Oh, well—it was only the first day of school, and a Wednesday at that. There was no need to panic. Yet.

The weeks rolled on. No Angela. I kept

praying, perhaps accusing sometimes, but seizing the promises of God as if my life depended on them. And, in a way, it did. God could not afford to fail me now—fail them now. He couldn't say no to such a request, could He? Would He?

I never removed Angela's name tag. I left her books in place. I continued to sit in her seat and lay hands on her desk. I reminded the staff to pray for her during staff worships. I answered the students the same way each time they asked where Angela was: "She hasn't returned to school yet, but she will be here." Where was my faith? It was placed squarely on God. Like a dog with a bone, I was going to hold on to that faith if it was the last thing I did. God had said to wait; I had to believe that was what He had said!

Turns out that He had indeed been trying my/our faith. As October rumbled to a close, my principal walked into my room one Thursday morning to let me know that Mr. Santos had been up to her office. Something had worked out, and the children were returning to school the following

Monday.

I was about ready to whoop and do cart-wheels in my classroom! God *was* real *and* could be trusted! He had come through for the Santos family. "Answered prayers," I assured my students who saw my struggle to contain my glee.

Sure, we had to play our part in help-ing these students stay. The vice principal followed later with a plan that would help their situation. After a quick consultation with God, I willingly threw my proverbial hat into the ring. After all, faith without works is dead, being alone (James 2:17, KJV).

On Monday morning my beloved Angela showed up. I introduced her to some stu-dents and presented her to others who had been her classmates the year before. My heart was warmed to see that God had ac-tually fulfilled His promise regarding His direct will. He also had made me/us a par-ticipant in the entire process. He had test-ed my faith and given me the opportunity to intercede as well as the privilege to say with a straight face and no hidden agenda that God is indeed real and can be trusted!

Without batting an eye, I say **Insert Praise Here!** In the past I had heard and read stories of people who persisted in prayer regarding objects of God's direct will and saw Him come through for them. Now *I* had a story that I could tell about God's faithfulness. Granted, the children had returned to school about six weeks into the first marking period. While I could not account for that time lapse, I could rejoice in earnest that they *did* make it in, anyhow. My soul was able to make her boast in the Lord (Ps. 34:2, KJV), because I could now say to all who cared to hear that I had *known* that God would bring them back to His school, and *that's why* I had prepared her desk in advance and had kept it so.

Needless to say, Angela was a wonderful fourteenth member of my class. During that year she worked hard and eventually blossomed as a reader. She ended the year on the Principal's List. The family has since moved to another part of the country, but when last I heard of them, the girls were still attending a Seventh-day Adventist school.

God had shown up and shone out in this situation after steadfast prayer and exercised faith. Although His answer was wait, and wait was what we had to do, God had not failed to do what He had said: "If we ask any thing according to his will, he heareth us: and if we know that he hear us, ... we have the petitions that we desired of him" (1 John 5:14, 15, KJV).

God is sure to answer our prayers when we pray according to His will. He has a direct plan for us, and sometimes it is in His plan to measure how great our faith really is. He will not always answer our prayers immediately, which gives us further opportunities to seek His face, to rehearse His promises—certainly not for His benefit, but for ours—and to stand our ground, to dig our heels in, to not give up, to persist in prayer. It has often been said that we tend to give up just on the brink of God's answers to our prayers. I have been guilty of that in many instances, but, God be praised, I did not flub that time!

Where is your faith? Be it the size of a

mustard seed or an avocado pit, hold on to it. Hang in there. Put God to the test. He longs to show Himself strong in your situation, just as He did for Angela and her sisters—just as He did for me!

Chapter 11

"I Have Gotten a Man from the Lord"

She was pregnant. Stunned silence. For her, at least. For a while she could not believe it. She was done with giving birth. After all, her third and *last* daughter was in the eighth grade; the middle one had already graduated from high school; and the first one was finishing up college. So she hadn't had the boy child—so what? There were worse things in life. She was happily married and loved her three daughters with everything in her. She was content.

But she was pregnant.

At the age of forty-seven, this was not

a choice she would have made for herself. Tongues would wag. She should be gearing up for menopause, not for swollen ankles and morning sickness! Her eldest daughter was old enough to be married and have a child of her own; instead, *she* would be the one changing diapers; *she* would be the one pushing the stroller, jostling with the car seat, walking the floor at night with a not-sleepy, colicky baby. She would have to relearn "new mommy tricks" after thinking that she had long graduated from all of this!

She was pregnant. This would change everything. This meant one more mouth to feed; one more future to plan; maternity leave, which meant salary interruption; and a laundry list of other implications.

She was forty-seven and pregnant. This would not be looked upon with favor by her medical caregivers, despite surging Hollywood trends. She was not one of those women with every avenue of medical care at her disposal. The risks were so high, too high. How could she have let this happen? What was she doing with a "belly" at this age?

One doctor bluntly articulated such sentiments. She had thought the doctor, as a female herself, would be a little more sympathetic, or at least sensitive. Unfortunately, this doctor was irate and pronounced doom upon this pregnancy if carried to term.

Feeling dejected, she left the doctor's office, her condition and the supposed implications weighing heavily upon her. She sought help from her friends, a group of church ladies with whom she dined each Sabbath and with whom she shared a bond that rivaled sisterhood. They prayed with and for her and encouraged her to trust God, because they knew that He would work all things together for her good (Rom. 8:28).

One of the ladies did some research of her own and found a better prenatal care center for the expectant mother, with a set of doctors whose bedside manners were far healthier than those she had encountered earlier. They carefully monitored her throughout each trimester and made her experience far more palatable.

But all was not smooth sailing. Ultrasounds revealed that she had intrauterine fibroids that were enlarged and competing with the growing fetus. This development compromised the safety of both mother and baby. Her age complicated matters even more. She refused the recommended amniocentesis, since to her the risks outweighed the positive outcomes. Rather, she chose to trust God with the care of her unborn child. She relied on Him to take her to term and to sustain her own health.

The news came that she would be on bed rest. This meant an additional interruption in her work schedule, which naturally would impact her salary. Steady work was not forthcoming for her husband; college fees had to be paid for both of her elder daughters; the family still needed to be maintained. This was not the best time to be off work. Why was this all happening at once? What were they to do?

She had no recourse but to let God take over, to let Him show Himself strong (2 Chron. 16:9). She could not see how it would all play out, but she trusted God

93

and talked often about that trust.

As promised in 1 Peter 5:7, God cared for her and her family during this time in ways that can only be attributed to God. He put people, friends, and opportunities in place to sustain them. She stayed on bed rest for the time required. Her maternity leave followed shortly.

She continued with her doctor appointments. As the time drew closer, concerns about the fibroids grew, as did the fibroids themselves. It was feared that a caesarean section might be in order. She prayed, as did her sister-girlfriends, casting all of her cares upon Him in keeping with 1 Peter 5:7.

D-day came, swift, fast, and sure. She was in labor. She barely had time to call one of her closest friends to let them know it was on. Her harried husband drove her to the hospital, where she was quickly received as her husband went to find parking. The staff barely had time to process her in; as a matter of fact, she never made it out of triage. Within 15 minutes of her arrival, at the age of 47 years and a few days shy of 11 months, she gave birth naturally to a bouncing baby boy. There were none of the telltale signs of trauma: no cradle cap, no visible anomaly. He could breathe on his own and was declared healthy by all counts! At any time, feel free to jump in and *Insert Praise Here!*

She needed surgery for the intrauterine fibroids. Ordinarily, it was a costly undertaking, but the same God who had provided her with a man child (Gen. 4:1) opened the way for her to have the surgery at the hospital where her son had been delivered, without additional cost to her—it was covered in the package provided by the hospital.

As she would tell it, the entire journey was God, all God! It was His providence at work so that her pregnancy was well timed. She believes that her seemingly belatedly born son saved her life. The fibroid that was removed from her was the size of a basketball! Had she not had her baby at that time at that particular hospital, she might not have had the details of her surgery work out in quite the way they did. It is also her firm belief that God has a very specific purpose for this boy. She bears witness to the fact that she has grown to trust God more than ever with her life's situations, ever since He showed up in such a marked way through this whole experience. Certainly she has a right to **Insert Praise Here!**

Today, more than four years later, were you to see this child, you would not be able to detect his uncertain beginnings. He is quite articulate, he is musically inclined, and he has a powerful memory. He has brought immense joy to his family and to all who know him. As for his mother, she has had the energy to keep up with him; her youth has been renewed like the eagle's (Ps. 103:5)!

It is no secret that often unexpected circumstances arise in our lives. When they do, they seem to be without cause. Our natural response in times like these is Where is God? or even Why me? Jesus Himself exclaimed in the throes of His suffering on the cross, "My God, my God, why hast thou forsaken me?" (Mark 15:34, KJV).

It is natural to experience such feelings during times of the unexplainable, times when we feel that we have no control of our circumstances. But it is at such times that God encourages us to cast our every care on Him, because He cares immensely for us (1 Peter 5:7). As ones who live in a sinful world, we are not without problematic seasons. But God has promised to be with us in these times (Matt. 28:20; Ps. 23:4; 91:15; Isa. 43:1, 2). He has also promised that, after we have suffered a while, He will establish and settle us (1 Peter 5:10).

We can rest assured of His absolute word. He who walked this mother through the challenge of her life and brought her safely to the other side can be trusted to do the same for you, no matter the situation. You can take that to the bank. That, in my book, is without dispute enough cause to *Insert Praise Here!*

Chapter 12

Grama's Legacy

(Tribute to Grama)

Grama was dead. The dreaded phone call came to my parents during the wee hours of that Wednesday morning, October 28, 1980. My dear maternal grandmother, Esther Theresa Melvonie Hugolyn Alexander (nee Kerr) had succumbed to leukemia at the age of 71. I still remember being numb after my father relayed the information to my siblings and me. Her death was not unexpected, but nothing had prepared me for its impact when it came.

"Grama," as we called her, was a wonderful woman. She was full of life and a tomboy, even in her latter years. Born to

Leah and David Kerr on September 23, 1909, the only girl among a passel of boys, she was a skillful horsewoman and could hold her own even among her rowdy brothers. Later she won the heart of my grandfather, Frederick Hannibal Alexander, whom she married and with whom she raised their three daughters, the first of which became my mother thirty-one years later.

Both Grama and Grampa were devout Seventh-day Adventists. They were instrumental in the early days of the Sangre Grande SDA Church. Grama was very active in church. She sang in the church choir, served as a deaconess, and was a devoted member of the Community Services department, then known as the Dorcas Welfare Society. The Dorcas ladies met on Monday afternoons. After school on Mondays we would walk over to the church to visit with them, but especially to see Grama. She would always have some treat for us. Sometimes it would be a little pocket change, but what we most enjoyed was her baked goods. Grama had a mean way with the oven! She made a molasses sweet bread that to this day is unrivaled in my book.

Grama would often come by to visit us at home; sometimes she would even stay over. She knew how to sew and would often make us play clothes and nightwear. Grama would take us out into the yard and play games with us. She showed us how to jump rope, among other things. I still remember the cricket bat that she carved out of wood for us. She brought it to us on her last stay-over visit. As the sun went down that afternoon and she took us inside after we had played with that very same bat, she said that this was the last time we were going to play together like this. I felt a sense of foreboding, but I was too young to understand what I was feeling or what Grama really meant. "I'm getting old and tired," or something to that effect, was her evasive response to our questions. Though we had wished for her to play some more with us that evening, we somehow accepted her explanation and called it a day. Fatigue had set in. She was experiencing what appeared to be the onset of a cold. In reality, Grama was battling cancer.

We went back to the welfare center the next week to look for Grama. The ladies reported sadly that she had not come that day—that Grama was very sick and might not be back. Again the sense of foreboding crept over me. I could not understand why we had not been told before about Grama's illness.

For our spring break that year, our family and another SDA family that was very close to ours went on holiday together in an old rambling summer house in L'Anse Noire on the north coast of Trinidad. We had a fun time together exploring the grounds and the many rooms of the old house. We enjoyed beach excursions and an exciting Sabbath at the Sans Souci SDA Church.

However, our blissful vacation was cut short by a message that was brought to us. Grama had become very ill. She had been hospitalized, and we needed to return to town. It was only then that we children learned the truth: Grama had cancer, and she had been given six months to live.

We were not allowed to see Grama at the hospital, but when she was sent home, we often visited her. I watched that vital, plump, independent woman waste away as disease and pain ravaged her body. Grama had a constant stream of visitors—relatives, neighbors, and church members—when she was strong enough to tolerate company. Her beloved brethren would sit with her, sing her favorite hymns, and pray with her. Some of the visits were very painful for them as they watched their treasured friend slip away from them. But Grama would sing along when she could, and more often than not she would speak words of encouragement to her visitors, many of whom, after her passing, continued to marvel at the spiritual strength of this woman of God during the darkest hours of her life. Grama was a friend of God, and she knew what was next for her. She had made peace with God and told us so repeatedly. She was ready to meet Him when He returned.

I never once heard my grandmother complain. Well, let me fix that: Not once did I hear her lash out at God for what had befallen her, though one day as we sat with her, she caught me/us staring, and, as pain spasms hit and broke her speech, she observed, "Look how ... all yuh ... grand-mother ... get" ("Look at what has become of your grandmother"). I hold back tears even as I write this some thirty-one years later. I cannot fault her for such a candid observation, even if it was meant as a com-plaint, because Grama was only human, and she did suffer greatly. Sin's effects saw to that. But Grama endured, even to the end. Before she died, she requested that the hymn "Someday the Silver Cord Will Break" be sung at her funeral. It was to be her testimony of sorts; the chorus de-clares, "And I shall see Him face to face, and tell the story—Saved by grace" (Fanny J. Crosby, 1820-1915).

It was hard to gaze into the coffin at the lifeless, emaciated body of my Grama as it lay in repose in the foyer of the Sangre Grande SDA Church that November after-noon. Many came out to pay their last re-spects to Esther T. M. H. Alexander. Much

of the funeral service was a blur, but I remember vividly a primary text of the eu-
logy: "Precious in the sight of the Lord is
the death of His saints" (Ps. 116:15). It was
comforting to know that, because Grama
had settled her account with God, her
death was precious to Him; that she had
died with the assurance that she would see
His face when He comes the second time.

It was hard to say goodbye to Grama,
harder yet to hear the sound of the dirt as
it fell upon her coffin, to look down into
that hole and know that she would be separated from us for the rest of our lives. We
buried her at the Foster Road Cemetery in
an east-facing grave—there's no way she
can miss Jesus when He finally pierces the
eastern skies!

Had Grama lived, she would have
turned 102 this year. I have often thought
of Grama, especially in my adulthood, and
even more so during the last two years.
I wonder what it would have been like to
have her around throughout my life. What
sort of guidance would she have given me?
Would she have been proud of how I turned

out? of all three of her daughters, who have stayed strong in the Lord to this day? of all her grandchildren who are steadfast in the faith and active in the service of God even as I write this? I have told God that I would love to be able to have conversations with her now; that I believe we could have been great friends—at least, I like to think that we would have been. I guess I will have to wait for a reunion under the tree of life, when we both have been made incorruptible, never again to be separated by death!

This was not by any means an easy chapter to write. Though thirty-one years have rolled over this dark event, though the God of comfort has been mightily with us, though we have carried on with life, the sting of death has left its mark. My grandfather never got over his grief at her loss and followed her ten years later. Since then we have lost other relatives and friends and have witnessed the pain of others as they have had to grapple with this disturbing phenomenon brought about by sin.

Human beings are not wired to cope with death, to accept its vicious invasion into our lives. Sadly, from the time our fore-fathers allowed sin into our midst, death has been passed on to all men, because all have sinned (Rom. 5:12). It is in stark contrast to God's presentation: obedience, which brings life; after all, "the wages of sin is death" (Rom. 6:23). Death is the result of the presentation of God's archenemy, the devil. He has lied to us about his offering. He made us think that rebellion against God would open us up to more knowledge than we could ever fathom (in other words, God was actually keeping things from us in order to dominate us); he fed us the bald-faced lie that we shall not surely die (Gen. 3:4, 5). Satan is an impostor and a thief (John 10:10)!

This is where this chapter turns a cor-ner. Think about the immensity of God's great love. God, in His foreknowledge, knew what would befall His beloved cre-ation as a result of sin, and so He laid a plan before the foundation of the world. It involved Jesus tasting death for everyone on the cross (Heb. 2:9), thus providing us with the free gift of righteousness and the ability to eventually "reign in life [eternal] by one, Jesus Christ" (Rom. 5:17, KJV). This is what my grandmother—and grand-father—died believing, and it was this gift that she—they both— accepted long before they drew their last breath. And I say, *Insert Praise Here!* For praise is due to the God who made this provision for them, for us, and for our loved ones who died in the Lord.

Death has lost its sting and shall one day be put out of commission for good! "So when this corruptible shall have put on incorruption, and this mortal shall have put on immortality, then shall be brought to pass the saying that is written, Death is swallowed up in victory. O death, where is thy sting? O grave, where is thy victory? The sting of death is sin; and the strength of sin is the law. But thanks be to God, which giveth us the victory through our Lord Jesus Christ" (1 Cor. 15:54-57, KJV). That day is coming soon. Hallelujah! By all means, *Insert Praise Here!*

"Therefore, my beloved [readers], be ... steadfast, unmovable, always abounding in the work of the Lord, forasmuch as [you] know that your labor is not in vain in the Lord" (1 Cor. 15:58, KJV).

***

This chapter is lovingly dedicated to the memory of my grandmother, Esther Theresa Melvonie Hugolyn Kerr-Alexander, as well as to her late husband, Frederick Hannibal Alexander. To her daughters—my mother, Phyllis E. McKenna (E. Lennard); and her sisters, Florence E. Grimshaw (Eric) and Melvina A. Springer (Errol): I hope that I have done justice in my short recollection of Grama's final days and the legacy she left us. Special thanks to you, Auntie Mel, for having borne the brunt of both your mother's and your father's palliative care. To her other grandchildren— Gillian S. Joseph (Ainsworth), Hayden L. McKenna (Nicaise), Arden S. and Tresha A. C. Grimshaw, who were even younger than we were during this time; and to Jared E. Springer, who missed it all, having been born after the fact: I hope this has given you some insight into the type of woman who was responsible for the wonderful mothers you—we—were blessed with. To my nieces—Kohren C. J., Kohrissa C. J., and Kohriese C. J. Joseph: this is a piece of your maternal history. You—we all—have a lot to live up to!

To whoever will read this chapter—indeed, this book—in the present or in the distant future: may you have found reasons to **Insert Praise Here!** even in the darkest moments of your life, in whatever circumstance you may find yourself. God deserves every ounce of praise that we could ever give to Him, but the praise to trump all praises comes from turning our lives over to Him for good, so that the reality of His gift of eternal life may be ours when He returns and kills death once and for all.

Maranatha!

The Tempest

Once in Bible times, on a day sublime,
Twelve disciples happily
At their Master's vote got into a boat
And headed out to sea.
And they sailed awhile in their finest style,
Not a worry or a care,
For the water was quite a favorite, 'cuz
They had many fun times there.
As they raised the sails, those twelve strong
males
Launched ahead into the deep.
Little did they know, taking turns to row,
That their Master lay asleep.
Suddenly the sky showed its darkened eye
As a cloud hid fast the sun;
The disciples stared, and their hearts were
feared,
For there was no place to run.

And the lightning flashed and the thunder
crashed and the winds did toss and blow;
And the strong rains beat on the small-boat
fleet,
Rocked it fiercely to and fro.
The disciples, sure as they lost the oar
That their lives were bound to end,
Searched in agony on the darkened sea—
Found at last their sleeping Friend
When the lightning flashed and the thunder
crashed and the winds did toss and blow.
"Master, help!" they cried. "Or we all shall
die!
Don't you care, Lord? Don't you know?"
Then the Master, stirred by their fearful
words,
Looked at them in love and said,
"Why so tossed about and so full of doubt?
Do not fear; have faith instead."
Then His face He turned to the storm
concerned,
And with mighty voice He cried.
He said, "Peace!" to the winds; "Be still!" to
the waves;
At His word they did subside.
Now there was a calm. It was quite a balm

On the sun-warmed, gentle sea.
As disciples sailed, their fears derailed,
Jesus told them quietly,
"Here's the lesson learned: Do not be
concerned
When life's ship is tossed about;
Once the Master's on board—your Savior and
Lord—
He'll be sure to work things out."

—*Bevan C. McKenna*
1/31/05

Knowing

I've heard a lot of things
I've seen many things, too
Many things I've experienced
I believe some things
I've been taught more things
But in all these things
I have learned this thing:
That there is nothing exceeding
That one thing—
Knowing.
Knowing that I am alive and
in my right mind
Knowing that while the world is by far
A very confusing and dark place
I can find peace, serenity
I can find truth in which to believe
Knowing that I am blessed with
Every breath I take

Insert Praise Here!

And that with each breath I can give
Thanks and praise
Knowing the One in whom I believe
The God of my praise
Knowing the depths of His love for me gives
me chills
Though I'll never grasp it all
Knowing that He made Himself sin
That I might be righteous
Knowing that He is faithful that promised
That He is with me always, that His purpose
for me is victorious, and
Knowing that one glad, fast-approaching day
He shall come again for me and we shall be
together forever ...
Knowing all these things
Makes my heart rich
Makes my soul glad
Makes faith into sight, hope into reality
Knowing all these things
How can I help but rejoice, exalt
And live for God, who is in all my
Knowing.

—*Bevan C. McKenna*
3/12/05

We invite you to view the complete
selection of titles we publish at:

www.TEACHServices.com

Scan with your mobile
device to go directly
to our website.

Please write or e-mail us your praises, reactions, or
thoughts about this or any other book we publish at:

TEACH Services, Inc.
P U B L I S H I N G
www.TEACHServices.com ● (800) 367-1844

P.O. Box 954
Ringgold, GA 30736

info@TEACHServices.com

TEACH Services, Inc., titles may be purchased in bulk for
educational, business, fund-raising, or sales promotional use.
For information, please e-mail:

BulkSales@TEACHServices.com

Finally, if you are interested in seeing
your own book in print, please contact us at

publishing@TEACHServices.com

We would be happy to review your manuscript for free.